CHILDREN ARE NOT CHESS PIECES

CHILDREN ARE NOT CHESS PIECES

The Game of Divorce

ELLEN SHAKER

authorHOUSE®

AuthorHouse™
1663 Liberty Drive
Bloomington, IN 47403
www.authorhouse.com
Phone: 1-800-839-8640

First published by AuthorHouse   07/16/2011

ISBN: 978-1-4634-1465-8 (sc)
ISBN: 978-1-4634-1469-6 (ebk)

Library of Congress Control Number: 2011912600

Printed in the United States of America

Any people depicted in stock imagery provided by Thinkstock are models, and such images are being used for illustrative purposes only.
Certain stock imagery © Thinkstock.

This book is printed on acid-free paper.

This is dedicated to the many people in my life who have contributed to the reason I feel it's necessary to commit these thoughts to paper.

Looking back on a road well traveled, though not always a smooth ride, it's a journey I wouldn't change. At its inception, we don't know what life has in store for us. We can only hope that we are good people who will make good choices for all those whose lives we will touch.

Contents

PROLOGUE

While the moral of a story is usually revealed after the story has been told, occasionally the significance of the moral is lost by the time we have reached the story's conclusion. And in this story, the finale is far too important to postpone until the end.

Perhaps the means by which each of us becomes the individual we may consider ourselves to be is why there are so many psychiatrists, social workers, and professionals of one kind or another who delve into a lifetime of rubbish that is unnecessarily dumped on us.

We cannot turn back the hands of time, but we can slow our children's dash into maturity that may occur during a divorce. As children, we want to be older than we are, dreaming of the things we believe age will enable us to do. Trying to guide your children throughout that journey is difficult when overshadowed by your shortcomings as parents.

Admittedly, there is no training for parenthood or divorce. We must all have more regard for each other as individuals, be that a spouse or a child. Our inability to develop emotionally can often be traced back to childhood. Knowing this, as we all do, makes it unconscionable to act out, as many of us will when headed for divorce.

It is, therefore, necessary for us to think past today, tomorrow, and even next year when a child's well being is concerned. In the blink of an eye, we are at our road's end. The voyage on which divorce takes us requires maneuvering feelings and situations to which children should not be subjected.

The truths of life are far stranger than fiction. The message of this story may be that we cannot undo many of the realities of life. How we handle them is directly related to how we are guided by our parents to do so, and in reality, that is the circle of life.

As you turn these pages, I will guide you through some of the nonsense that became my childhood, adolescence, and adulthood. It's a bird's-eye view of the damage that was done after two otherwise "normal" people got through with me.

As you glimpse into some of the things said and done, you may find yourselves wondering who would do these things. You may believe yourself incapable of such behavior. But trust me, in reality, we are all capable of many of the same stupid moves as my parents made. Perhaps I can get to you before you turn out to be one of these stupid people too.

Children are a gift from God, one of which not all of us is worthy to receive.

REFLECTIONS

I have been here.

I am the product of a divorce.

I am a stepchild and a stepparent.

I have been divorced.

I have the dubious distinction of experiencing divorce not as a spectator but as a participant from all points of reference. My hope is to communicate some of what can happen during a divorce when words, actions, and deeds are wheedled by thoughtless contributors.

Perhaps divorce is the litmus test for us as parents, possibly even as human beings. It is an event that, for a time, alters all our sensibilities. The particulars of divorce make it a hard pill to swallow for the children involved, even if it occurs when the children are adults. For many, divorce can challenge us to the core of who we are and, as a youngster, who we may become. There is a delicate balance of love and loathing that must never be heaped on our children at any age.

We are vulnerable when it comes to love. We lay down our heart only to have it dashed on the rocks of divorce. In the certainty that no one chooses to be hurt by love, we inevitably play some part in its employ. Not so for children. We bring them into this world with joy and hope for their future. We need to make their lives a journey of wonder and discovery, not an adventure into the perils of life by way of our selfishness.

Reflect for a moment on the times you dislike most about your own upbringing. Be honest because you know there are at least few instances and perhaps you still think about them. Magnify these through the acts you may perpetrate on your own children during a divorce and imagine where it may take them in life. In using the analogy of children as chess pieces, it may well behoove us to take a step back and recognize that everyone's life is not a game. Take a minute to assess what's really important.

Relationships with anyone ought to be based on communication. Without it, the connection between people can easily vanish. When it occurs to either you or your spouse that there is a problem that's serious enough for you to consider divorce, you may already be at the point of no return. Understandably, with the pressure of your life falling apart, it's improbable for cooler heads to prevail. Consequently, life can easily get out of control, and we say and do things we later wished we had not.

Divorce often negates our sense of concern and caring for someone we once gave our heart and life to, and the hurt is like no other. It can twist our emotional responses, and we can be manipulated into selfishness we may never have known we possessed. In the face of this prospect, it is imperative that, in the best interest of each of you and more importantly your children, you reach deeply inside the love you once shared. Make an effort to utilize that love to resist vengeance and careless ridicule in a situation for which there is no victor.

Each of your wounded egos will heal in time, and you can emerge a renewed and possibly an even better mate. Sadly, the result of your domestic melee is likely to exist in your children's emotional makeup for a lifetime. Step back for just a moment, knowing that your life together is coming to a close and agree to be concerned for the life unfolding for your children. When each of you considers your behavior during your marriage and how you are now dealing with a divorce, you may see some of the things that contributed to where you both are at this time. If these things didn't work out in a better moment, how will they work out for anyone during a divorce?

Now is a period that involves making complicated choices, perhaps ones that affect everyone for eternity. Children are at the heart of making a divorce work out as amicably as possible. So dust off your egos, put away your need to exact a settling of scores, and protect your children from yourselves.

As I reflect on my life and the road behind that is far longer than the one ahead, allow me to share some of my experiences. With any luck, my experiences will shed light on what happened at the often-thoughtless hands of my parents. These were the people—people just like you—who were supposed to care for and protect me but so often did neither while involved in their divorce game and its aftermath.

And so, the chess match begins.

Children Are Not Chess Pieces

Children are not pawns to be moved around to save the king and the queen in the game of life, but they are often used during a divorce to "check mate."

Even if you do not play chess, I believe we all have some basic knowledge of the crux of the game. Chess is a game of thought, concentration, and skill. It is a test of someone's ability to contemplate past the move he or she is about to make and read the other player. That ability to read the other player and what his or her next move might be can play an invaluable role in surviving both a game of chess and a game of divorce, especially concerning your children's well-being.

Some of us are masters of the game, but even masters can be defeated. Truth be told, there are no masters in the game of life. From beginning to end, we really do spend most of our lives in a learning process of

6

one kind or another. Just when we believe we have it all figured out, something happens to make us realize we don't.

Though hundreds perhaps even thousands, of books and articles have been written on the best techniques for child rearing, contrary to popular belief, it's a secret to which no one possesses an answer.

I don't pretend to have the answers on the best way for you and your spouse to maneuver your way through the maze of divorce. There are, unfortunately, no rules for this game. Divorce disrupts the lives of everyone involved, most of all the lives of your children. In actuality, all you may need is bit of common sense, respect for what you once had as a couple, and the ability to put the needs of your children before your own. And yes, I know this is a tall order at best.

If you have been unfortunate enough to be a product of your parents' chess match, this may offer some solace: If you are about to enter into your own chess match, you need to sit back and read this book. Perhaps it can be a syllabus of sorts for a more gratifying life for everyone affected by a divorce.

Just Being a Kid

We remember when just being a kid was wonderful. There were no worries and no problems, and the trials and tribulations of life had no real impact on us yet. Our parents were people we could always depend on to make any circumstance better. I know I thought my parents could walk on water, as most of us do. All too soon, though, it would come to pass that the water evaporated, and I discovered there was no bottom to their buckets of misery.

The circumstances that bring us to the decision to divorce are different for each couple. But in the end, the result is the same: Children are in the middle. I wonder if, as adults, we believe we are showing our kids how much we love them by how much we fight over them. The more my parents fought, the less I felt loved. Even as a kid, I think somewhere inside me, I knew no part of their battle was really about me.

There have been a few times when I wondered what I could have become with a supportive family behind me. Many people who know me casually often think of me as confident and tough, maybe a bit arrogant. But those who know me intimately know I am really quite different. While I may not cry in front of you, it's quite easy to make me do so, if only inside.

Unfortunately, early on in my life, it was necessary to become or at least appear self-reliant, able to depend on myself rather than the frequently less capable adults around me. I have sometimes compared myself with a snake lying in the sun. When bothered, I'll find another sunny spot, but when bothered again, I'm going to bite. The "I'll bite you before you bite me" mentality is a defense mechanism I felt I needed, though one that has not always served me well in life.

Far too often, this kind of mentality, or something much more serious, is the end result for children of divorce. Mom and Dad are so consumed by the details of the divorce itself and building a new life for themselves that the kids sometimes become baggage. Whatever you, as the adults, choose to do with your new lives, keep in mind that your kids come first.

As it turns out, life is incredibly complex. Divorce or no divorce, kids require care, concern, and guidance. You both may need to remove your respective heads from your posteriors and plot a course your kids can actually follow, not one they will want to run into a ditch.

THE SONG

I contemplated whether to write this book for some time, as it seemed it would be an overstatement of the obvious. As my life ticks away, though, I feel almost a responsibility to share some events I hope will give even a few of you insight into how to navigate the rapids you are about to careen over. I guess, to put it bluntly, I want to point out ahead of time how brainless divorce can make us. More significantly, this may actually help you form a strategy for what not to do during a divorce.

One day, while listening to the news, a thought came over me. Time and time again, we hear disturbing stories about people spiriting their children away to foreign countries or taking their entire family's lives and their own while being embroiled in a divorce. While extreme, it happens many more times than we should be comfortable with.

Loving someone who does not love you in return is a devastating feeling. That feeling should never be at the expense of anyone's life or overall welfare. Unfortunately, though, divorce is, in reality, so often about possessions and retaliation, not about love.

Make a note: I will say over and over again that divorce is not all about my feelings and me alone.

Close your eyes for a second and think about your first encounter with love. Life was an awakening of all sorts of feelings and the exhilaration of being with that person. You thought you would never be able to live without him or her.

When the relationship ends, it seems as though someone has torn your heart from your chest, and you feel you cannot go on without the person you loved. You get through it and go on to find love yet again, that next person to love whom you cannot live without.

With this in mind, why make any relationship go on unnecessarily and keep each person from moving on to find that next love? While in the midst of my parents' divorce, a couple more of my mother's divorces, those of several friends, and, of course, one of my own, it seems we as adults should have evolved to a point where we were able to dissolve a marriage with a degree of decorum. But not so!

While at some point we must accept that our life is, in the end, our own responsibility, the people and the things that make us who we are play an important though silent role in our development. No one really wants to know how he or she came to be a particular type of person, nor does anyone have an opportunity to tell his or her story about the journey. As parents, we cannot be with our children

11

at all times, and the world can be an unforgiving place. Be it by design or mishap, when we sign on for parenthood, we are accountable for our children's every need and must give them the tools to make the best life choices possible.

I believe we are all born with a song in our heart and a soul full of love. While it may be born in each of us, the song is easily silenced by selfishness and indifference. Don't be the person who silences a child's song.

Consider for a moment a song for which you alone have the words. While involved in the dance of divorce, may each of you really listen to the words of the song you are about to compose. Inevitably, it will be a tune that resonates in the lives of all who are compelled to bear the weight of its conclusion. Life can hold many wonders and, at times, countless hazards.

Be the one who forever encourages your children's songs.

Kids Aren't for Sissies

If accolades are what you think kids are about, perhaps you should consider raising show dogs instead.

When we marry, it's usually assumed that we will have children. That's certainly demonstrated by someone asking at the wedding reception when you're planning to have a child. You probably think, "Hey, could you at least let me digest the wedding cake?"

Rather than having a child because it is what's expected, how about we really contemplate all that is a part of being a parent because being a parent is the most important job any of us will ever have?

Children are not dolls. They cannot be put back in the toy box when you're done playing with them. Unfortunately, we neither know nor are prepared for just how difficult or, for that matter, how thankless parenting can be. We go from being the most important people in our children's lives to varying degrees of insignificance to the most important again. Stuck somewhere in between, we also waver between being the smartest people to just clueless. For children, these changing views may be about security versus freedom and are just part of the growing-up process. We, on the other hand, as the grown-ups, should know better than to do and say many of the things we will in the name of love and in the folly of divorce.

Parenting is a skill learned by doing. It may be a bit easier for you if you have good parents, although good is a quality not easily assessed. Perhaps too many of us feel that when mistakes are made in the parenting process, they are someone else's fault, and we should not be held accountable.

Unfortunately, righting mistakes, while a parent's responsibility, is not always as easy as it sounds. There are no absolutes, and what works for one person may not work for another. It may be our job as parents to figure life out even though it is complicated and impossible to always know the right thing to do. But you must figure it out because your children's lives will ultimately be influenced by your decisions.

Divorce complicates "figuring things out" on so many levels. We just want what we want. Unfortunately, we know we can't always get what we want. We must be able to put our wants aside to some degree and think, if even for only a minute, what's the best thing for the kids.

There are no awards for being a good parent, nor are there demerits for being a not-so-good parent. Regrettably, even the not-so-good parents think they've done a first-rate job. There is pride in knowing you have done your best and have possibly shaped someone who will go on to do great things—or someone who will go on to do something he or she likes.

Children emulate what we say and do. I know we may think they really don't hear us, but in the end, they are always listening. Consequently, it should be apparent that we really do lead by example. For that reason, what is it you'd like your children to take away from your example?

LET THE MATCH BEGIN

I think each of us believes we have given our marriage our all. It is, however, far too easy to become overwhelmed in a world that seems to have run amuck when it comes to working at marriage.

Disappointingly, even our best attempts at happiness are sometimes fruitless. No one wakes up one day and thinks that he or she is going to try to fail at something. The reality of life is, in the end, it's just not always easy or what we think of as fair. And when it comes to divorce, there seems to be no rationale for fair. Don't compound the negativity of this situation by waging war on each other.

Frequently, even after we have tried our best to keep a marriage together, it's just better for all concerned to let it go and move on—and move on is what we must be allowed to do. There is a time for unfathomable hurt, resentment, or maybe even rage along with a host of other emotions. These emotions need to be part of how you get through the process of divorce.

We all have, maybe while shopping or at the beach, observed people and wondered what they see in each other. There's no need for an explanation why

16

they may really love each other or be on the verge of divorce. Who knows what makes an ideal match? I guess that's the reason cars comes in different colors: We don't all like the same things.

Just as we sometimes cannot imagine why others are together, we may look at our own spouse and wonder the same thing. It happens—we grow in different directions and need to reassess our mate.

We need to recognize that we should not stay in a bad marriage for too long. When a marriage is done, it should be dissolved somewhat amicably. I implore you and your spouse to make every attempt at civility and empathy regarding what you once had. Divorce need not be a fight to the death, though more frequently than not, it's just that. Possibly, it is because we cannot let go of the need to win as you might in a chess match. Maybe winning is simply one of those human flaws. While we all like to win, a divorce should be treated like what it is: not a competition but our lives as well as that of our children.

Consider for a moment all the wonderful things that brought you and your spouse together. Also reflect on the things that have brought you to this place of considering divorce. Regrettably, you can never go back to the starting place of your love. Instead, a respect for the love that gave you the gift of a child should never be far from your consciousness.

It's essential to consider that while you may no longer be spouses, you will both always be parents. "Mom" and "Dad" are powerful words. The uproar in someone's life during divorce is far reaching and affects all aspects of life. Often, because so much is at stake, we throw caution to the wind and leap into the divorce process with no regard for their outcome. Unfortunately, once certain things are out in the open, we cannot retract them. So act responsibly, not irrationally.

In a chess match, the worst-case scenario is that you lose. In real life, losing may have more far-reaching ramifications when children are used as the prize. They may be destined to be the real losers. In any game, there can be only one winner, so allow the real winners to be your children.

Save a child—it really is worth the effort.

WEDDING BELL BLUES

Weddings are a milestone event. It's the day many young girls dream about. There are thoughts of gorgeous gowns and a handsome groom, beautiful flowers and elaborate cakes. Family and friends from near and far come to be part of this fabulous day. It's no wonder then that getting married adds so much worth to our lives, that proverbial "be all and end all."

If you have never married or you waited until later in life to do so, people somehow see you in a less positive light. This is especially true if you are a woman and, God forbid, no one has asked you to marry him. That means there must be something wrong with you.

It's no wonder then that each of us—men as well—go into marriage perhaps somewhat unrealistically. Our expectations about marriage may have been blown out of proportion thanks to earlier hype surrounding the wedding itself. When the party is over and we get to the reality of living as a couple, for some it's a direct ride to the bottom of the hill.

It's disturbing to learn about the lack of value many of us have for marriage. Recently, a couple childhood friends and I were discussing marriage. One of them shared that as she was about to get married, she said to herself, "I'll just get divorced if this doesn't work out the way I want." I guess it did work out since she and her husband have remained together for some thirty odd years.

Despite the fact this couple is still together, this is an unfortunate commentary for all too many that view marriage with such uncertainty. Failing at marriage, undoubtedly, is not part of any rational person's conscious thought process because most of us believe the fairy tale that love conquers all.

Alas, soon after the gifts are put away, we need to get down to the business of life as a couple. It can be a huge adjustment, and life can unintentionally derail us. We get caught up in our jobs, friends, and families and therefore forget to communicate. Then there are those high-profile marriages needing a prenuptial agreement and what seems like a plan for its demise before it begins. Perhaps marriage should be on a ten-year contract basis that will enable us to renegotiate our terms. Today, it seems we are all so bombarded by failing marriages that we may unconsciously be hardwired for failure.

In marriage, there is one truth: It is always a work in progress that needs to be tended to daily as you would a garden. You must give to get and while there are times one person gives more than he or she gets, you need to find a balance that appeases both partners. I deeply admire chronicles of marriages that have survived and even flourished during times of crippling injury or dire despair. It is, in my estimation, a testament to what marriage should be. All too often, though, we are far too young or immature or, in reality, just make an unwise choice as a spouse.

Subsequently, there is the addition of children to the mix. Children, while wonderful, really do complicate relationships. Frequently, we have children because our parents want grandchildren, and it's what society expects of us. Granted, if we all waited for the optimum time to have children, we never would have survived as a species.

We do, nonetheless, need to be prepared for what having children involves. They are a challenge that we are not always geared up for or mature enough to manage. It is, in fact, a job that is yours for a lifetime and a responsibility that should not be taken lightly. Often, when a relationship is on fragile footing, we choose to have a child, believing for some ridiculous reason that a child will bring us closer together. Especially under these circumstances, nothing could be further from the truth. A child's life is nothing to be trifled with and should never be used as a bargaining chip.

And so begins using children as the pawns in our little chess match.

Who's an Idiot?

I'm not a doctor, nor, as the saying goes, do "I play one on television." I certainly do not have any professional credentials to advise anyone on child rearing or divorce. What I do have is an education through the school of hard knocks. It's the personal experiences that have led me to feel the need to convey not advice but the nuts and bolts of what divorce can do to your children.

Early in life, as so many of us are today, I was the product of divorce. As a matter of fact, I'm the product of more than one of my mother's divorces.

Take time to consider how your anger cannot only destroy your life and that of your partner but also that of your children. You, as an adult, can make conscious decisions as to how a divorce plays out in your life. Sorry to say, your children are the pawns in this chess match. They are at the mercy of you and your soon-to-be-ex-spouse, caught in the middle to be moved about at your will and used as leverage for money and affection.

While we think of ourselves as being above this sort of behavior, when the floodgates of emotion open and the smallest incidents are blown out of proportion in an attempt to demoralize the other person, you, too, are making choices you might regret.

People have been getting married for centuries. With all our education, you'd think we could come up with an easier way for its dissolution. We can easily turn into idiots when it comes to the end of what began as one of life's most extraordinary events.

Think for a moment of someone you know or a celebrity whose divorce has played out in the media. The things that become important during a divorce are bizarre. There's the chair one of them can't live without or the cemetery plot for twelve that's "mine." One of them needs thousands of dollars a week to live or one partner says, "Give back that kidney I gave to you."

The measures to which people will resort to exact a pound of flesh is mind-boggling. Sadly, the immeasurable damage that can be done to children during this little game may turn out to be more life changing than you and your spouse could ever imagine.

So listen up, Sparky, this is you. Getting divorced is no sleigh ride, especially if there are a lot of assets involved. It's never an enjoyable experience, even if it is your choice. When divorce comes as a surprise, it's even more devastating. Life deals us things that are not part of our plans. This is the reason you as the adults need to step back, take a breath, and have a strategy that is about your children and how to help them, as well as each of you, to get through this life-altering event.

The end of any partnership is cause for anger, despair, and feelings of betrayal. After the dust has settled, each of you gets to go your separate ways and begin a new life. While that's great for each of you, where does the best interest of children enter into all of this? They are not free to make a choice of any kind about their lives. Often, we are so caught up in our own hurt and anger; this is one of the last things we consider.

Trying to digest divorce, as a kid of any age is, at best, an endeavor. Life experiences that may help, even a little, may not have happened yet and when Mom and Dad put on their best "idiot suits," it becomes all the more difficult to cope with what has happened. The children's lives become the never-ending barrage of "he said, she said" and the slightest indiscretion is now the event of a lifetime.

Before you get to this place, the place of no return, please stop for a moment and think. Think about how we are all appalled when we hear news of children being spirited away by one parent, never to be seen again, or out of vengeance physically abused or even killed. These sorts of actions seem to equate to the idiotic thought process of "if I can't have the kid, no one will" and is somehow a solution for one more "idiot" thinking only of him or herself.

Then and only then do we call for someone's head on a stick.

In a not-so-obvious way, you may be on this very same road. We wrongfully think of abuse as only broken bones, cuts, and bruises. Abuse is well disguised inside so many of us, often leaving wounds that never really heal. It cannot be reiterated enough: Words can pierce even the toughest skin and cause us to second-guess ourselves, perhaps for a lifetime. For some people, these hurts resurface and, as is well documented, can fester and lead to horrible acts on themselves as well as others. While this is extreme, can you take chances with your children's lives?

Everyone deals with the death of his or her marriage differently, and each of you really needs a mourning period. In your heart, when all is said and done and the air has cleared, take a look back and ponder why either of you reacted how you did. Children, on the other hand, do not have that luxury, and they are often left to deal with the aftermath of the irresponsible behavior that ensued between their parents.

So before either of you warm up that idiot suit, realize you and the other idiot can still make this chess match amicable, and the winner does not need to take all.

Love can be a fragile and fleeting emotion. Each of us will love many people in varied ways during our lives. The exception here is the love of a child, which is truly like nothing else.

As you begin divorce proceedings, you must never lose sight of the fact that your children are a result of your once-undying love for each other. While that love may have died, we must never be willing to allow ourselves to indulge in our own self-pity so we lose our children in the battle.

Let this be an attempt at saving each of you from your own inner idiot and sparing even one child senseless sorrow at your hands.

To a Path Undiscovered

Unlike today, when I was a child, it was not commonplace to have divorced parents. I believe I may have been the only kid, or at least one of a very small minority of kids, in my graduating class whose parents were divorced. I consider it one of my life's most overwhelming events. Because it was not common at that time, no one was really prepared to deal with my feelings—certainly not my parents, my teachers, or my friends or their parents.

In fifth grade, I remember a boy calling me the "black widow," and, as a freshman in high school, because by then my mother was on husband number four, a teacher asking me, "So what's your mother's name this week?"

These are perfect examples of the stupidity we are capable of as adults. People don't always know enough to remain silent, and children poke fun at things they don't understand. Once you have said something stupid, it is impossible to take it back. We can fix almost everything with duct tape, except stupid. So I hope you can see the importance in thinking before you speak, something there is far too little of in life, even sans divorce.

The reality is it's more poignant to avoid stupidity during divorce as well as life after it. So much of my life, even as an adult, has been about being stuck in the middle of my parents' affairs.

My parents have been deceased for many years. While each of them was perhaps in their own way an OK parent, I don't languish over them no longer being alive. Their lifelong bickering, supposedly on my behalf, robbed me of the feelings I envy in other people's relationships with their parents. Isn't this an ugly thing for a child to feel about his or her parents?

As the adults, you cannot put your children out there in a world that most of us are ill prepared to live in to drown in a sea of emotions, perhaps floundering for a lifetime. Don't use your children as your personal sounding board or punching bag. Your hurt should not be theirs. Remember your life is not their responsibility, but their lives are yours. The events that have caused you and your spouse to divorce need to remain between the two of you.

Why is it that otherwise outwardly bright people feel the need to put their entire life onto their kids' plates? Telling your kids about the other parent's infidelities or sexual hang-ups, etc is a definite taboo. Sharing because it's fair does not apply here.

Obviously, each of you wants your children to know your side of the story, but at what cost? What you communicate about the other person may in fact

tell more about you than him or her. You might wa
to consider the ages of your children and just wh
really needs to be told to them. More is not bett
As difficult as it may be, try to explain things yo
partner has done in a way that leaves blame out
the scenario. Lord knows there's enough of it to
around between the two of you.

At the end of the day, does it really matter to t
kids what happened, and do you absolutely kn
for yourself that certain events occurred? The blar
game is a futile one; we all contribute to the go
and the bad in our marriage. Though it is hum
nature to blame the other person, this is a time
step back for a moment, reflect, and take stock
yourself as well as your spouse. Keeping that
mind, try to temper the "truths" you share with t
kids. Try as we might, some of those truths are p;
of our memories forever.

The furor of the woman scorned lived within I
mother for the remainder of her lifetime and v
acted out on me for my lifetime. I have hea
endlessly about my father's affair with the wom
who'd become his wife in what seemed like
nanosecond after my parents' divorce. My mothe
need to feel blameless was neither informatior
needed nor information that, in my eyes, did I
mother any good in the long run.

Sharing some personal details can make childr
feel inadequate and unloved, among a host
other feelings they may lug around throughout li

29

Children should not have to sort out or deal with certain pieces of personal information about you or your former spouse. There are things that are not your children's business.

Let's use this scenario as a case in point: I was in my forties when my father took his own life. While I was staying at their home for several days afterward, his wife felt this was the time to unburden herself of so many of their intimate details. I heard all about their sex life, etc and her version of how she and my father became involved. I really thought my head would burst.

After a life filled with this sort of nonsense, I thought not much else could easily astonish me. Well, just when you think you've heard it all. I remember thinking, "My God, woman, my father just committed suicide and this is what you feel the need to share with me?" OK, at this or any other time for that matter, was when I really needed to know my father was a lousy lay? Yes, two more lifetimes at least could have gone by without these tidbits. Too much information! Ouch, my head!

I know it's been said there are things that should remain a mystery, and much of the information that was shared with me as both a child and an adult certainly fell into this category. Adults assume children are unaware of the context of the turmoil going on around them, but they grasp so much more than we give them recognition for.

Many years ago, a friend wanted to have her ex-husband's parental rights taken away for what were valid reasons. I campaigned for her to rethink her decision because I knew from experience how easily her plan could have backfired. When a child thinks that he did not see his father because you stopped it, all the good you have done gets washed away in the child's thoughts, and he feels you were the cause of his separation from his father, not the person at fault. As it turned out, she did nothing and as her son got older, it became apparent to him just what a loser his father was. Her son eventually wanted nothing to do with his father, but that decision was one for him to make, not her.

When we marry, I think most of us really believe it will be forever. Unfortunately, far too often, forever has a shelf life. The reality of living all too often has a way of changing the fairy tale we think it to be. When this occurs, it is our duty as parents to shield our children from the unnecessary hurt our thoughtless and purposefully vindictive actions can and will cause. A child is like a sponge that absorbs everything in its path.

Isn't it our responsibility to try to make as many of our children's memories as possible, a part of life cherished, not trash to be hauled within us for eternity?

MY OWN PARENTS DEAREST

When I was a child, kindergarten was purely the start of the school process. You were not required to be able to read or write, be an athlete, project S&P stock trends, and know the college you would one day attend. You were just there to be a child and learn to take direction from someone other than Mom and Dad and become a bit more social.

Early in my life, my father spent hours teaching me to read and spell words like "hippopotamus" and "encyclopedia." Lord only knows when a five-year-old will be called on to spell these words, but whatever.

It was my father who made several of my Halloween costumes, carefully disguising my red hair. In those days, whoever passed out the candy just needed to know who you were. We would take rides in the car, just my father and I, and sing the same little songs he'd taught me. It was something I'd come to really miss when my parents separated.

My mother, as most mothers, was the disciplinarian. She, unlike many women in the early fifties, worked outside the home. While getting ready each day to go to my grandmother's house, in the winter my mother often warmed my clothes on the oven door. I helped her bake sugar cookies for Christmas and make Milky Way crosses at Easter that she'd decorate with frosting flowers—the usual sort of kid stuff.

After the divorce, at great financial strain, she provided me with baton and dance lessons and always dressed me very nicely. She was never the warm, fuzzy sort and wasn't big on displays of affection. It was perhaps a telltale sign for my parents' upcoming divorce. While I'm sure she did, I just don't remember her saying she loved me.

Before they got divorced, my parents got together regularly with a few other couples on Saturday evenings at one particular couple's home. No one else had children at the time except my parents. I was one of those "premature" births. You know, the first one comes any time and the rest take nine months.

From what I can remember and what people have told me over the years, these get-togethers may have been the beginning of my parents' problems and my mother's leap into problem drinking. It seems my father had a bit of a roving eye.

I'm not sure if my mother ever consciously wanted children. Obviously, it had happened, but it never happened again. I've enjoyed, I guess, being an only child. Having no other point of reference, it seemed just fine and gave me the ability to amuse myself.

33

Being able to entertain myself proved invaluable for much of the rest of my life.

It always seemed odd that, as her only child, my mother did not remember what day of the week or time of day I was born. When I was about twelve, she loutishly informed me one day that if abortion had been legal when she was pregnant, I wouldn't have been born. Wow, there's a sharp stick-in-the-eye moment for you.

This story, another little family jewel to be shared with a therapist in later years. What followed was what I thought under the circumstance was a strange, astonished look of horror, and it appeared my therapist was about to fall off her chair. Then came that ever-present therapy question, "How did that make you feel?" Yeah, I was overjoyed for my mother to tell me she'd just as soon have flushed me down the toilet as have given birth me. What sort of ludicrous question is this from someone who is supposed to be well educated and capable of helping you? How in the hell did the therapist think it made me feel?

By the time I was eighteen, my mother was deeply immersed in alcoholism, and I had long since been the "mommy." One day, while I was trying to get her up for work, we had an argument, and she threw me out of the house. I went to live with a friend and her parents. When I called my father that evening, it was as if I'd called to tell him I'd just gotten a puppy. His nonchalant attitude upset me immensely. I was crushed at his lack of concern and cried for days. Not until my mother had harassed him on the phone for a couple weeks did he extend his home to me. By that time, I'd have gnawed off my own foot before I'd have gone to live with him.

Obviously by this time, dear old Dad was not exactly a winner either. He remarried immediately after his divorce from my mother and frequently moved from town to town and state to state. While I saw him regularly in the beginning, soon living in another town or state made the visits more infrequent. It often seemed my parents could not put enough distance between their new lives and anyone who might have known each of them during my father and stepmother's first marriages. As time went by, it seemed my father and I knew very little about each other. In the end, we were strangers. Even though each of you may go on to another life, remember you had another family first.

And then there was my father's letter right after I'd been divorced from my first husband. He felt it necessary to point out how disappointed he was in me and that, at forty, he thought I was nothing. Here was yet another poignant statement from one of my "parents of the year." My father and I did not speak for some time and except for him writing me a somewhat apologetic letter, I'd probably have never spoken to him again.

There are volumes to be told about both my parents, but that would be a book in and of it self. The past is the past, and I can only make the future better. It was and is up to me to do this. As mentioned previously, don't make your kids your whipping post. It should be clear to even the densest of you what damage this sort of behavior can cause for children.

In an attempt to save myself, I can only believe that my parents' need to lash out at each other by ultimately using me was the only way to relieve their own hurt. I guess in some wars, a few battles must be lost. So tag, I was it!

A Day for All Days

So the decision to divorce has been made. The day this all comes to fruition will remain in everyone's memory for a lifetime, so please consider this: Some fifty years later, I still recall the day my father left our house for the last time as though it happened only a split second before. I can still tell you what the furniture we had looked like, its exact placement in our living room, and every word my father said. It was my own day that lives in infamy.

This all took place on a blustery November day, the day my childhood came to an abrupt halt. I guess, in the true altruistic eyes of a child, you always think your parents will love you. Sorry to say, in a divorce, your love for your children can become their worst enemy.

The day my father left seemed like so many Sundays before. My family got up, went to church, stopped at a neighborhood store that had the best hard rolls, and headed home. After breakfast, my father fixed the oven and began to prepare dinner, as he often did on Sundays. After what seemed like an amicable meal, he told me to go outside because he and my mother needed to talk. That, sadly, was the last talk they ever had.

As I recall, it didn't seem like talking was something they had in common then or ever again. I walked around outside for what seemed like an eternity and was freezing. I was locked out of the house, so I knocked on the door to see whether I could come in. Then and there, "eternity" really kicked in.

As I went into the living room, my mother was sitting on the sofa crying. My father had me sit in a red chair in our living room, in a spot where a chair was never placed again. Those earth-shattering words—"I am leaving"—came spilling from his lips. "I don't love your mother anymore, and I am going to live somewhere else."

There was no consoling me or taking a moment to explain anything. He already had a bag packed and off he went. I've often thought about how he could have broken the news that he was leaving and made it easier for a nine-year-old to grasp. I guess there may not have been any easy way. It did, however, always seem that was his way and to hell with telling his child that he didn't love her mother any more. I think it somehow translated in my head that he didn't love me any more either.

As the door closed behind him, I didn't know what life had in store for me.

I remember being numb, too young to really grasp the impact of what had just happened, though life has a way of slapping you in the face very quickly. After much crying, I was sent off to school the next morning. My mother insisted I go. I guess she really needed some time to herself to attempt to digest what had happened to her. Of course, I cried at school, and my teacher took me out to the hall to find out what the problem was. Even today, I feel badly for this poor woman. She had no idea what to do or what to say.

Well, life goes on and you learn to handle what it deals you, something I learned to do throughout life from then on. If you do nothing else, remember that during a divorce, you will make indelible memories that last a lifetime.

Ostensibly, the day my father left may have been the last day of the rest of my mother's life. As the front door closed behind my father for the last time, someone should have unearthed a piece of ground and tucked her under it, for she was never again any use to herself or anyone whose life she touched.

Perhaps we all need to take a step back from life and its ups and downs to look at ourselves introspectively. If divorce is an inevitable part of your existence, don't have just a plan but a good plan. Obviously my father had an exit had a plan, but trust me it was not a good one.

While there will never be an easy way to let your children know a divorce is about to happen, you must try to make it as painless as possible. It won't be easy, no matter how kind you are. If children are involved, you and your spouse cannot just call the kids together and tell them in a way that may hurt everyone later. While it is a decision that must be made by adults, you can't expect children to really understand the concept that you've decided to divorce and one of you is leaving them. You have just sprung an incomprehensible concept on your children.

I think people, on the whole, spend more time researching what vehicle they are going to buy than the effect some of their words and actions will have on their children. It is amazing to see how we have evolved and yet how inept we still are when it comes to the fundamental, commonsense aspects of everyday life.

I hope that in death my parents have come together at last to see the aftermath of their hurtful behavior in me. I, like so many people, occasionally wonder what could have been.

Anyone Can Have a Child

Even though no one intends to fail at any part of life, it does happen. When it happens to our marriage, it affects so many people. After all, look at all the effort and money that goes into a wedding. All too soon, though, we sometimes discover marriage is an escape from some demon. I'd come to find that true many years into my first marriage, as I believe it was for my mother. We both may have been ultimately trying to escape our respective mothers.

My mother had been married before my father, an event I learned about by accident from a newspaper article I found hidden in our linen closet. Inadvertently, I mentioned the article to a friend's mother, who, as any nosy neighbor would, questioned my mother about it.

Throughout my life, my mother's fury over my knowledge of her first husband was always a bit curious to me. You know that adage about protesting too much? It has often made me wonder if that man was really my father. I know he lived somewhere near our home, and my mother seemed so protective and secretive about it.

As an adult, I met someone who had known my mother when she was married to this man and who said that I looked like him. My mother went ballistic. She screamed and yelled that I did not look like him—again perhaps a bit of overkill. I know so few details about when my mother was with this man, although I do know she was pregnant with me when she married my father.

I have vacillated from time to time, seriously and not so seriously entertaining the idea of exploring whether my mother's first husband might be my father. However, there has been enough drama in my life, and I venture to speculate it is an irrelevant point at this stage of life anyway.

As I have matured, most of the unpleasant feelings toward my parents have waned. When I look back, there has been damage done I can never reconcile with anyone except myself. This is why it is so important to be mindful of your actions and the words you use. They truly do last forever. We cannot rewind the clock to make these actions go away. Why not try to make sure they never happen in the first place?

My first marriage was to someone who was a controlling egomaniac and, in retrospect; I believe I metaphorically married my mother. As I have been told, while not necessarily what you want, this behavior is what you know.

I did very much want to have a child with my first husband. We talked about this before our marriage, but since he already had a child, he did not want another. After a couple of years dating, I broke off our relationship. In an effort to get me to change my mind, he enthusiastically promised that we would have a child. I'll readily admit my heart listened to what my head really knew would never happen. Of course, the idea of a child all changed very quickly after we were married.

I have to confess as time went on in our marriage, I knew having a child with this man was never going to be in the best interest of a child. While it's something I occasionally think about, I knew in my heart what was right for a child. Having a child is not about you and what you want; it is about the child and what is best for him or her.

A few years ago, my adult stepson apologized to me since, because of him, I do not have a child of my own. The thought never occurred to me. It hurts me to the depths of my heart to think he feels that he was responsible in any way for me not having a child.

For most of us, having a child is the result of marriage or a relationship, though not everyone is cut out to be a parent. Bearing or fathering a child does not a parent make!

I don't believe we give nearly enough thought to the singular most important event in our lives. There's the decorating of rooms in special motifs, fawning parents, and your thoughts of nothing else accept how you will bring up this little being. We get so little education from anywhere in life to be a parent, and nothing else in life prepares us for its totality. Anyone can have a child.

Only when you get divorced does the law in many states often require you to attend a parenting class. We get directions for everything we purchase, from how to put a breakfast food into the toaster to how to use tweezers. Not until we have had an adequate amount of time to screw up a child does someone think we need to be taught how to care for one. Go figure!

Parenting classes were not part of divorce in the 1950s, and I'm not sure they really need to be today. It seems to be the cart before the horse thing, you know? First and foremost, when you have a child, you need to realize there no longer is just you. When you are having a baby, if you'll notice, you are rarely the one who receives gifts. And, for a pretty lengthy time frame, most activities revolve around the kid. Why, then, should it not occur to us the absolute importance of a child? And with that in mind, why is it we are so willing to pull out all the stops to hurt someone who is an integral part of that child's life, even at the expense of the child?

For its time, my parents' divorce seemed particularly nasty. Each of them, as well as the woman my father left my mother for, worked in the same place. It seemed everyone knew my father and his coworker were having an affair—except, of course, my mother. My father was an electrical engineer in a textile mill, so getting phone calls late at night to take care of some issue while not very common was not out of the ordinary. Oddly, I do remember those calls becoming more frequent some time before he left.

Very shortly after my parents' separation, I met the new woman several times in what I believe were supposed to be perceived by me as happenstance meetings. I've always found it amusing how dense adults think children are. I certainly hope my father never believed after the first time we just "bumped" into this woman that I didn't recognize why she was always there. Even as a kid, you catch on quickly. Though I was only ten, I wasn't dense.

In the blink of an eye, this woman was part of my weekly visits with my father. Looking back, I didn't get to spend much time with my father alone then or ever again. It would be some time before I would learn that she had two children, considering they were never with us. I was told they were "away at school." Later in life, I found it particularly disturbing to learn her children's "school" was in fact an orphanage.

Yes, Daddy, you found yourself a real winner!

ED AND DOT

Looking back as an adult on a childhood conversation with my father about him needing to find the things he was lacking at home makes me understand why he felt this way. Lord knows I'm more than aware of how difficult a person my mother was. In the grand scheme of things, I believe she was essentially a good person but on many levels was a sorrowful soul.

Sadly, little did Dad know what that new life he left us for had in store for him. Imagine his surprise to discover just how much his new wife would be like my mother, only worse. Lamentably, in the end, he felt taking his own life was the only alternative. It is a bit disconcerting to know that, in light of the heartache suffered by all, he exchanged my mother for someone who turned out to be tantamount to his worst nightmare. Perhaps the fact she was able to essentially abandon her own children should have been a warning to him.

There was a succession of very unpleasant times with this woman. I can honestly say I have never known anyone who could go from zero to mega bitch more quickly than she could. The slightest things sent her into a seething, spewing rage with anyone around her. I didn't have many occasions to stay at their home as a kid, but when I did, wow! It always amazed me as I watched my father turn into an acquiescent pile of mush when she began a rampage. Without her around, this seemed so out of character for him.

During the beginning of their marriage, my father and my stepmother did well financially. While not wealthy, they never worried about where their next bowl of soup was coming from. Unfortunately, money would be a great source of friction for them in later years. Money always played a far-too-important role throughout their lives. My father had some health issues, and they were at odds for some time about his possible future needs and how these needs would affect their wealth. As fate would have it, money was more important than his health.

It was Christmas morning, and I called to wish my father and my stepmother happy holidays. My father answered the phone, and we engaged in a short conversation. When I asked to speak to his wife, she bellowed from the background something about not wanting to talk with me and she'd call me later.

As she eventually told it, she and my father got into a huge argument over her not talking with me. Sadly, it was really a continuation of a conflict about money and his health they'd been having for the past several months. He stormed out of the house, shouting something about killing himself, and she told him to go ahead. She told me he returned once later in the afternoon, and they continued to argue. He left again and, sometime during the night, returned to their home, taking his own life in their garage.

While throughout a good deal of my life after he and my mother divorced our relationship was disconnected, this is a call I can assure you I never want to experience again. In hindsight, it wasn't hard to figure out that the fighting that went on for so long between my mother and my father had really been about money. The helplessness of this upsets me each time I think about it.

While my parents were separated, my father was supposed to pay the mortgage on our house, at least until the divorce was final. He, I'm sorry to say, did not. Shortly after the divorce, a sheriff came to the door with a twenty-four-hour eviction notice. My mother begged and borrowed money from anywhere and everyone she could so we could remain in the house. I was abhorrently offended, upon my mother's death, when my father said he'd given the house to my mother for me. Obviously, he was oblivious to my knowledge of what had really occurred. How ironic that he'd come to discover that money isn't everything. I guess in the end, the set of standards you live by are the same ones you die by.

I have an unwavering feeling within me that my stepmother knew what was happening in the garage that night and did nothing about it. Perhaps it was her actions while I was at the house that caused me to feel this way. "Actions speak louder than words" screamed in my head for a long time. In fact, it was their neighbor, whom I'd never met, who called to tell me my father was dead. My stepmother did, at some point, get on the phone with me for just a moment in what I'd come to sense was a well-orchestrated act.

It's difficult to describe why, but my stepmother's actions sort of spoke volumes for me. I flew down to my father's home with a feeling in my heart I have never felt before and hope never to feel again. When my stepmother and I went to the funeral home the next day to make the arrangements for my father's cremation, she chose to have his ashes sent to me. She was quite adamant about not wanting them. Odd, wouldn't you say?

I am a very visual person; I need to see everything. I asked the funeral director to see my father before he was cremated. My stepmother did her very best to discourage this and had no idea why I wanted to see his body. She even told the funeral director that it had not yet registered with me that he was dead. I certainly was aware he was dead. As his only child for whatever my reasons, shouldn't I at least be entitled to see him one last time?

When the funeral director called a couple days later, my stepmother took me to the funeral home. She vehemently refused to go into the room where my father was lying. I realize everyone deals with this sort of situation in his or her own way. It just felt, especially under the circumstances, such a cold, unfeeling response to the death of her spouse.

Later in the week, I got a call from one of the detectives who were at the house the morning my father's body was found. He said he needed to speak with me, which really freaked me out. My stepmother took me to the police station where we were ushered into a conference room with the detective and an officer from the property department. My stepmother asked if my father had left a note. It seemed peculiar that the two officers looked at each other rather strangely and one handed her a copy of my father's note. It read, "Now that you have everything, I hope you're happy."

I was horrified by her reaction. She screamed, "This is what I get after thirty-four years?" and continued to loudly rattle on. The authorities and I left her yelling in that room while the detective took me to a small room and asked me what I knew about what may have precipitated my father's death. I explained what I knew, and that was that. It was most disconcerting to answer his questions, and I asked whether they thought something else had happened. The detective explained it was just a formality in the investigation.

Never let it be said that we stray too far from our comfort zone. Even in death, here was one more hissy fit as a send off for you, Daddy. Just then another detective knocked at the door, asking when we'd be finished because my stepmother was out in the lobby pitching another fit. When I went out there, she was dramatically draped over the back of a chair in a scene reminiscent of an Academy Award performance.

It's awful that my father, or anyone for that matter, felt suicide was his only way out. I am truly sorry for how selfish this may seem, but after all the other crap he and my mother put me through, I have one more bit of baggage to drag though life.

As an example of how I was always in the middle of my parents and stepmother check this out. My stepmother had recently, unbeknownst to my father, obtained a safety deposit box to which one of her nieces had the other key. She did tell me about it, though I was sworn to secrecy. My father also had a safety deposit box for which I had the other key. My stepmother hadn't known about my father's safety deposit box; however, he told her about it on the day of their last argument.

Upon my arrival at their home the day of his death, my stepmother almost immediately took me to my father's safety deposit box to find out what was in it. I believe my father had given taking his life some thought. He made me the beneficiary of his 401k and had left the paperwork for that and some cash in the box for me.

My stepmother took me to her box and gave me a diamond tennis bracelet. Her exact words to me in the bank were "the things your father left you and this bracelet are all there is, don't expect anything else because you won't get it." I hadn't gone there expecting anything, never mind what I got. Somehow that wasn't the most appropriate time for any of this to happen.

To add insult to injury, this "devoted wife" was apparently in quite a hurry to be free of any reminders of my father. She sold his truck out of the garage two days after I got there. We thought he was inside the vehicle when he took his life. I later found out from the police report I requested that he was found under the tailpipe.

Obviously, in order to sell my father's truck, it needed to be cleaned out. Guess who got to do that. Perchance this was the telltale hint of a guilty conscience? I must tell you that getting inside a vehicle you believe your father has just taken his own life in was probably the single most difficult thing I have had to do in my life. It was really creepy.

By week's end, as I was preparing to leave for home, my stepmother had given me every picture, cufflink, pen set, etc she could gather together to rid her life of what seemed like any trace that my father existed. Within days after my leaving, she cleaned out and gave away all his clothes and, I guess, was really done with him.

And, in the end, this was the person for whom my father left my mother and I and then gave up his own life. Life does, in the end, sometimes hold as many ironies as truths.

MEMORIES

No matter how we try to rid ourselves of them, some memories seem to have a life of their own. Be they good or bad, they are part of who we become. I am now in my sixties, and my stepson lives near the exact spot of the conversation with my father about how you fall out of love. Even today, some fifty plus years later, each time I pass that spot, the conversation resonates in my head as if it took place yesterday. As a kid, I really hated what my father said. As an adult, I do get it, but as a child, they were words beyond my comprehension.

Your need to exact retribution for a broken heart reaches farther than you can ever imagine. It can affect the decisions your children make on all levels of their lives. The quality of relationships girls have with their father often affects the sort of men they are attracted to. Mothers, in turn, have such an impact on a boy's life and the relationships he has with women. Abusive relationships, at any level, have effects on your children that they can be burdened with for life.

Divorce is an ugly word that, by definition, is a legal dissolution of the marriage bond. There is nothing in that definition that pertains to children. They were not the reason you fell in love. Why then do we use them to try to destroy that love and the other person at any cost?

In the midst of the upheaval of divorce, we lose sight of our own truths. We are all participants in the events that lead us to this place. We, at some point, should be able to recognize our own foibles as well as those of our spouse. We either make adjustments for them or perhaps, as many of us do, blame the other person for them.

One of the principal things to remember when getting divorced is that there are three sides to every story: your side, your spouse's side, and the truth. Remember that you and your spouse are the only parts of this union that are splitting up. Your children should not be asked to make a choice between the two of you. It can leave many women to think that because they are often the chief caregivers after the divorce that it gives them some right to expect the child to love them more. This was the obvious choice for my mother. Any gift or gesture from my father was perceived as a personal attack on her and some attempt to undermine her ability to care for me.

In particular, there was the legendary coat my father and my stepmother gave me for a Christmas gift. When I got home with it, all hell broke loose. My mother was incensed and called my father, screaming and swearing that she didn't need his whore to buy her kid a coat. I did not really like the coat let alone look at it as one less thing my mother needed to provide.

It was the beginning of a lengthy tug of war between my parents. Well, really among my mother, my father, and my stepmother, with me once again in the middle. I never wore that coat, but it was plenty shop worn going back and forth from my mother's house to the car when my father and my stepmother came to pick me up each week. There was my father yelling about why I was trying to give the coat back. Then I got a beating from my mother when I got back home with the coat. This stupidity went on far into the summer and beyond.

I hated that damn coat!

My father's child support checks were always a bone of contention as well. I want to note here that it was twenty dollars. I'm well aware that the value of money was quite different when I was a kid. Still, it was twenty dollars.

He regularly sent the check unsigned. I guess he thought my mother couldn't cash it then. Well, she just signed his name and off she went. On a few occasions, he rather nastily asked me why so many of the checks were cashed in a bar. Hey, Ace, how about you take this up with my mother? It's not like the check was made out to me. I was a kid with no say as to where it was cashed or how it was spent. I do remember getting into trouble for saying pretty much the same thing to him. Have some gumption and go to the person you have the problem with. Why expect your children to be the go-between for either of you?

This sort of foolishness spilled into both my teenage and my adult years. I was not allowed to invite my father to my high school graduation because, of course, my stepmother would have attended and Mom was not having that.

When my ex-husband and I were planning our wedding, which we paid for, my parents were at each other's throats for weeks. My mother was so troubled that my father would give us more than she could financially. Whatever my circumstances with her, though questionable at times, it still was her, not my father, who had really provided for me until then. So why shouldn't he have done more if he could (and he could)?

The evening of the wedding, my mother caused such a scene about the gift from my father and my stepmother that I threw my mother and her husband out of our home. Was this really the day for hoopla about some history between my parents? It should have been a joyous day about my husband and me. I'm sorry for selfishly thinking my parents could act like human beings for something as inconsequential as my wedding.

Initially, I was quite satisfied with the gift my father and my stepmother had given us. However, in an effort to make her point, as was her way, my stepmother told my husband and I that their gift was substantially less than they originally planned. This was supposedly because of the fuss my mother caused. I really have no idea what my mother and their gift had to do with each other.

Once again, can we see the pattern, the one where I continued to be the last consideration? I know in my heart that for my father and my stepmother, it really came down to the money and an attempt at humiliating my mother—not that she really needed any help in that area. Color me jaded, but I don't believe for a minute they ever intended to give my husband and I more than they did. In the continued oblivion of my father and stepmother as well as my mother's behaviors, I was never destined to be the winner in their little games. Why change history at that point?

So, as you can see, there will be many auspicious occasions in your children's lives that each of you has a right to be part of. While these occasions belong to your children, they are part and parcel of parental memories too. I cannot imagine many children who want anything less than you being part of these times. Regardless of your feelings, each of you should be able to conduct yourselves as adults, put aside your stance on things for a few hours, and be there for your children.

Repeat after me once again: It's not always about me.

THE JOURNEY

These stories are merely a few in a very long list of "pleasantries" that followed along what I've come to call my life.

While some of the loves in our lives will come and go, our love for our children will not. Though we expect their unconditional love, we need to be able to give it in return. I wonder how many of the books and articles written on divorce and child rearing have been written by folks who have actually experienced these things. Unless you personally have had the misfortune of having made this journey, many of the incidences I relate may seem almost comical, maybe even fabricated. I might not believe some of them either had they not happened to me. It does sort of sound like a movie, doesn't it? Unfortunately, you can see how absurdly we can behave. My husband often tells me he wonders how I've managed to turn out even something close to normal—whatever that is!

If a spouse dies, there are many ways to explain that to a child. While it takes time to heal from that hurt, for the most part, you do. Divorce is different in that the child is constantly reminded of the person who is now only a visitor in his or her life. Weekly visits are hard because they often are only for a few hours. It's tough to have influence as a parent on someone you see for such fleeting intervals.

Then there are those arrangements where custody is split between the parents for six months at a time or, worse yet, a week at a time. For whatever it's worth, these are arrangements I find unconscionable for children to be subjected to. These arrangements are for the parents' convenience (or imposition of one parent against the other) and have little or nothing to do with the children. They have everything to do with the two morons who must win at any cost. Many of you are barely able to sort out what to do with the silverware, never mind what happens to kids.

I want to preface the next section with and make very clear that what I say about any of the next scenarios is my personal opinion. They may work for you and your children.

There was an article in our local newspaper a time ago about a couple and how they were trying to work out each of their time allotments with their children. It went on to say how they mapped out this time sometimes a year in advance. Perhaps this seems admirable, but let me continue. Their plan designated each of them to fifteen to fifteen and a half days per month with the kids—in two and three day increments. The kids sometimes left for school from one home and returned to another. This may have allowed both parents time to have a hand in raising their children but, in the end, just what was this arrangement about? The father went on to say that he didn't sign up for fifty percent custody when he had kids. Well, how about this: neither did your kids.

Imagine being asked to have two different lives, including different schools, friends, food, and pets, maybe even having to live in two different towns and states. Who was the idiot who thought this was a solution? Though trust me, seeing one parent once a week isn't much easier. I know of a couple that lived together for a few years as if nothing was wrong in their marriage. They did not even let their families know they were really living sort of separately. Perhaps this wasn't the best choice either because kids are far more astute then we think, but I do, at the very least, admire their attempt at being concerned for their children.

If and when each of you remarries, the kids are going to have another family situation to deal with. How easy do you think it is for your kids to deal with some man or woman being put into the Dad or Mom role? Often there are other children to be introduced into the scenario—yet another possible problem. After all, the kids don't get to choose any of these people they are now being asked to "love." We often are so bitter about the other parent's new spouse that we try to poison our children against this person. What harm can be done by your child being allowed to develop a loving relationship with the new spouse and children? After all, there can never be too many people to love our children.

Let's face the facts. There is no good answer to what may be the best way to handle a divorce. Children need both parents to be an integral part of their lives. You each must rise above the things that have brought you to divorce in the first place. As difficult as it may be, you both need to remember that while this journey did not begin with children, it is ending with them. How you handle the divorce can exact a toll on children that is life building or life crumbling. Be open and think of ways that give each parent some vacation time, some holiday time, and so forth. For some of you, you can even think of it as a little well-deserved time off. In the end, the kids might even thank you for it.

We all need to consider for a moment that the journey of life must be rocky enough to be a learning process, smooth enough to be enjoyable, and long enough for us to appreciate its worth. Our accomplishments during this passage are not nearly as important as the consequences they may leave behind.

Here's to your journey.

Send in the Clowns

Now here's an actual complication and the real oxymoron: divorce and common sense. Common sense seems to be something you either have or you don't, but come on, is anyone that dense? You are about to enter into something where there is no sense, no common sense, and nothing makes sense. Put aside what you see in the movies or on TV. Life's just not that simple. Appreciate that it is real people whose lives are at stake. So dig deep, I know there's common sense of some sort in there why not use it, what could it hurt?

And common sense gives way to, well, this must be the place where they say, "Some of my best friends are attorneys." I want you to know I in no way mean any disrespect to the legal profession. It is their expertise we seek in divorce situations to enable us get to the most equitable outcome.

In an ideal scenario, we would be able to hash out the details of our lives to the best end for all concerned. After all, it was our life and who should know what's best for us but us. Frankly, while that should be the case, the dissolution of a marriage becomes far more complex and takes more cunning than any chess match. It is at this judgment that it becomes necessary to hire attorneys, and often here is where the real drama begins. Consider the reality that you are an attorney's occupation, not necessarily his or her concern.

Here is a bit of advice. First and foremost, hire the best divorce attorney you can afford. Obviously, the complexities of the division of property, child custody, and the like require more knowledge of the legalities than we have. More often than not, we need some disinterested party to intervene and sort out our life.

Attorneys are often blamed for the outcome of a divorce, but you must know they are only getting one side of the story: yours. A divorce is not the time to be anything but totally truthful. Do not—I repeat, do not—keep any secrets from your attorney. You do not want to get to any court proceedings and have some surprise sprung on your attorney by your spouse's attorney. Your dirty laundry will get out. With that in mind, spill your guts.

Perhaps this is the most important time to be truthful with yourself as well as your attorney. You need to keep in mind, though, that the aftermath of this situation will be your life to live, not your attorney's. Sometimes an attorney's intervention causes as much discord as it settles. Though, in reality, it is our own inability to view the magnitude of the situation that causes most of this discord.

Once all the court appearances are over and the attorneys have been compensated, you'll be left to begin a new life. Let it be one that you can begin by being able to look at yourself in mirror and know you did all you could to make the best choices for yourself and your children's lives. Things often have a way of working themselves out better than you might think.

For my parents, even after their divorce was final and they each had gone on to another life, the battles continued. I don't remember or am not sure what many of the battles were all about, but the billable hours mounted. Over the years, they battled again and again and certainly none of this was the attorney's fault.

When I was in seventh grade, after visits with Dad, I missed school almost every Monday and, as time progressed, Mondays often became Tuesdays as well. After his visit and nonsense, I'd go home and the battle with Mom began. She would shrew on, and I spent hours vomiting. There were many visits to more than one attorney's office for my parents' talks and shouting and blah, blah, blah.

After some time, the school called my mother, and I was sent to the doctor to determine why I was missing so much school. The doctor was our long-time, no-nonsense family doctor who was familiar with my parents' divorce situation. I remember her chastising my mother about what the two of them were doing to me. I was on the verge of an ulcer. I remember feeling somewhat vindicated because someone was finally sticking up for me.

This sort of out-of-control behavior can and often does go on for years. An attorney can only act on the information he or she is given. You as the client hold the reins, so slow your little clown car down and be in command of your own life. Strive to keep the stupidity in check with facts. It is not that difficult to know your limitations, being mindful of the means to an end. As long as you allow someone else to be in control, you have no choice in the outcome. Money and possessions are always at the root of the problem. Embattled parents also seem to view children as chattel. Stuff is just stuff, and you can get more. Where do you get a new, undamaged kid? At some point, it should be apparent that no one is getting much out of your continued battling.

If we could possibly separate what was, what is right now, and where we want to be, it might help in the outcome. You may not be thinking about beginning a new life at this point, but you will build a new one. Each of you will go on to create some sort of new life for yourself. It is difficult, but if you can move on without being too contemptuous from all that has happened, a new beginning is sometimes just what the doctor ordered.

Keep in mind each of your roles in this mess and that this is the only life each of you has. Let it move on with thoughts of rejuvenating your view on love and relationships. Our children learn from what we do and especially what we do in distasteful situations. In the end, the clowns get into their little clown cars and go on their way. Where are you going?

As You Continue On

And so a new life must begin. Keep in mind, the aftermath of all the ugliness that has transpired between the two of you will take a toll on your children. Always keep in mind that your choices, good or bad, were never the choices of your children even though they may pay for the consequences.

Each of you will go on to find a new love and a new life. Everyone needs and deserves a second chance at happiness. Frequently, though, the first family seems to get lost in the sauce. As the weekly visits with my father tapered off, in time, it really did feel like his second family became more important than me. It's a tough pill to swallow, although one many kids have to.

My father's new family went on many great vacations, and I was never included. When I was sixteen, I went to visit, and they took me to a wedding. While at the wedding, my father and my stepmother introduced me by my name rather than, as my father's daughter because they didn't want anyone to know either of them had been married before. It made me feel pretty worthless as a daughter that they didn't want anyone to know I existed. It's no wonder I have sometimes felt I was an outsider in my own life.

Then there was the dating years I endured with my mother and the succession of losers who paraded through my life. My mother's family had a predisposition to alcoholism. My grandfather was an alcoholic, as was my mother and all her siblings. In fact, none of them but my grandfather lived to be fifty-five. So the men she attracted were also alcoholics. She'd marry twice more after my Dad and the last one was, well, you decide.

One Saturday when I was almost thirteen, my mother and I went to visit my aunt. She lived in a pretty large city about thirty-five miles away from our home. My aunt had two young children, aged two and six months. My mother and my aunt went shopping and left me to care for the kids. This little excursion turned into four days with me alone with my aunt's children. It was a very frightening experience. I'd babysat before many times but never for that long or somewhere totally unfamiliar.

My mother was married at the time to husband number three, and he finally called the police when we did not return home. My mother and my aunt were found in an apartment over a bar that my aunt hung out at with the man who rented the apartment. Soon after this incident, my mother got divorced again and this guy, who would soon become husband number four, moved in with us.

I've known many women who never remarried because they had a daughter and they were afraid someone might harm her. Well, I guess that was not a concern for my mother, though it should have been. Her fourth husband was ten years younger than my mother and let's just say a real jerk. Even today, I cannot fathom what she ever saw in him. Obviously, at least part of the attraction was that he was a drunk too. He spent way too much of his time trying to get into my bed. My mother knew I slept with the door locked. She'd caught him in the backyard several times pleasuring himself outside my bedroom window.

I am grateful for knowing enough to keep myself safe, so nothing ever happened. I refused stay anywhere alone with him and did my best to keep out of arm's reach. There were many indiscretions perpetrated on me by my mother over the years that I can forgive her for but never this. Unfortunately, she was one of those women who felt even a bad man was better than no man.

My mother and I never spoke about anything regarding her fourth husband. It seemed that as long as she didn't know whether he'd ever done anything to me, it was all right. She just didn't want to know. And yet this is another reminder of the overwhelming consequences a parent's choices can have on a child's life.

So while you go on to a new life, do so with some caution. Not everyone you'll find will be like my mother's fourth husband, but beware. Make the best choices you possibly can. No one expects you to dry up and blow away because you have kids. However, when you have children, you really need to operate under a different set of parameters. Unfortunately, life holds no guarantees. We just need to try to make the best choices we can. This is especially important when it is the second time around, and there are children to complicate the mix.

If you remarry, try to do so using all the information life has given you differently than you did the first time. Sometimes, divorce strikes a second time, a third time, or more. Often, there are more children added to the scenario. Was it that enjoyable that you'd want to endure divorce again or put more children through it?

Blaming anyone for his or her shortcomings holds no merit because, ultimately, you are in charge. We make countless life choices based on many of our previous life experiences. We often emulate the poor choices of others and suffer the same perils. I have made my fair share of mistakes, and I have strived to learn from them. I know I, as well as you, will continue to make mistakes. Hopefully, they're just not the same ones.

Perhaps there are no mistakes but lessons to learn and live by.

COLLATERAL DAMAGE

My own experiences aside—well I guess this is still my experience because it concerns my stepson. The clear-cut damage done to him by his parents is absolute and irreversible. As an adult, he has made strides in his life far beyond, I think, even his own expectations. He and his wife are wonderful parents and she, too, is a product of divorce.

My stepson spent so much of his youth and early adult life as part of the walking wounded and, on many levels, he still is wounded. The games that have been played with this kid's head are beyond measure. His parents are two people who had and continue to, even today, have the gall to win at any cost. The unfortunate result is a man who, on the outside, seems as hard as nails while on the inside continues to be a hurt and angry little boy.

I know the drill myself only too well. As a matter of self-preservation, you develop a hard shell to keep hurt at bay, though you are anything but strong. Unfortunately, it is a foible that follows you throughout life. Many people think you are abrasive or unpleasant in some ways because you do not allow them much leeway. It is yet one more cross to bear in a life that often has been anything but fair.

The ability of my stepson's parents to wound him, even as an adult, is incredible yet continues. The selfishness exhibited by each of them is a perfect example of the point I'm trying to make. From the moment we are born, we are a product of so many influences outside our control. In divorce situations, we are at the mercy of folks who have only their own petty needs and concerns in mind.

In retrospect, I know there will always be people who are so narcissistic that how their choices impact others does not matter to them. It's a shame some people choose to have children. I'm troubled that parents can be so clueless and unconcerned about the results of their foolishness. The mind-boggling aspect is that these people really believe they have been good parents. I certainly know that I, too, could have done some things differently and better with my stepson

His father and I petitioned the court for custody when my stepson was twelve, though it was not much of a struggle. At best, it was an exercise in the appearance of caring exhibited by both parents. The prize to be won was something different for each of them, and my stepson was not it.

In retrospect, the whole procedure was far beyond belief. My stepson has several older half siblings, so his mother conceded pretty easily. The behavior of the court official that interviewed each family member was ludicrous at best. It takes quite a bit to shock me, but this guy gave new meaning to the phrase "a real piece of work."

My ex-husband was sixteen years my senior, so the court official wanted to know why I had married him. My reply was because I loved him and the court official commented, "He married his wife because he had hot pants and could not handle money." Perhaps this is a perfect example of how family situations are handled by our legal and social systems. I left the interview that day in a state of bewilderment, thinking how the fate of many children rested in that man's hands.

In the end, my then-husband and I were granted custody of my stepson. It was at this point that, while it was never said out loud, my ex-husband's actions screamed it loud and clear to me—"So you wanted a kid, now you've got one." Soon his son's actions spoke to just how loud and clear it was to him as well. Medical, school, or some legal situations, they all pretty much were my responsibility to handle. There were trying times, as there are in raising any child, and it took quite some time for my stepson to get his life together.

After everything that happened, he has turned out to be a man of whom I am very proud. He is a business owner, a good husband, and a wonderful father. He makes it his business to be an active part of both of his children's lives. Saying "I love you" to them is a daily occurrence, something he did not hear from his father.

My stepson and I sort of grew up together. I'd just turned nineteen, and he was about to turn three when his father and I began dating. We have always had a very close relationship, and it continues to be one I cherish today. My present husband and I are thrilled with our role as grandparents, along with the "real" grandparents. While God did not grace me with a biological child, I could not love my stepson more. He didn't have to come from my body to be in my heart.

Still, I am troubled at the thoughtless actions of both his parents that continue to take a toll on him. We talk regularly about his relationship with each of them, and it makes a hole in my heart that there are some things I cannot make right for him. I cannot reiterate enough how absurd conduct leaves everyone to deal with lasting effects for which there is no cure.

When you divorce, obviously a new life begins. If each of you remarries someone with children, you become a stepparent and while you will never take the place of a parent, you are still a role model. In these situations, you may be the only voice of reason in a kid's life. Take the opportunity to do with the child the things you hope your kid's stepparent is doing with him or her. That "it takes a village" saying should apply, no matter whose kid it is.

We, as adults, are here to protect and nurture children no matter to whom they belong. In the end, swallowing your pride, if you will, is the best thing for all the children involved.

I'd like to share a note my stepson wrote to me on a Mother's Day a few years ago. Of course it made me cry knowing he felt like this, and this note is more valuable to me than any gift he could ever give me.

"Ellen,

Your guidance has immeasurably influenced all that I have done and all I will ever do. Your sprit is indelibly imprinted on all that I have been, all that I am, and all that I will ever be. You are a part of all that I accomplish and all that I become. And so, it is that, when I help someone, your helping hand is also there.

When I ease the pain of a friend, they owe a debt to you. When I show a child a better way, either by word or example, you are the teacher once removed because everything I do reflects values I learned from you. Any wrong I right, any heart I may brighten, any gift that I share, or any burden I may lighten is in its own small way a tribute to you.

While you did not give me life, you are the spring from which flows all the good I may achieve in my time on Earth. For all that you are and all that I am, thank you for being my mother.

Love your son,

Bill"

Now tell me there's a dry eye after reading that!

I share this not to be self-serving in any way. It is rather an effort yet again to drive home the point of the consequences our behaviors have on our children. If the truth were told, there is fulfillment in knowing anything I have done possibly had a positive effect on someone's life.

Knowing that your actions have such lasting ramifications makes them that important. So don't just be a parent but the force behind an astonishing person—someone you have made into a kind person with feelings for himself or herself as well as others. Allow him or her to develop into all he or she can be without being encumbered by the selfishness that you may have unfortunately instilled in him or her.

It's wonderful to see my stepson turn the unpleasant behaviors he and his parents shared into the loving and nurturing manner in which he behaves with his own children. He and his wife took in his nephew, who is the son of one of my stepson's half brothers. Their attempt to help him is a way to give the boy a chance at making better choices when at the mercy of parents too selfish to do the right thing.

And yet I know my stepson struggles with many demons, as do so many of us who are the products of divorce. We just try to be more than those from whom we came.

THE PLAN

There are no idyllic ways to predict how someone will react to some of the information he or she receives about a spouse and the life that was shared prior to a divorce. Life seems to come at you in a million directions. Some of this information may actually floor you.

I used to own a lingerie store and learned many things about people's sex lives and lives in general than I needed or cared to know about. Be guaranteed that many of the things purchased were not for the customer's spouse.

You'd be surprised at the number of people who don't know these sometimes-disturbing aspects about their spouse, so be prepared. You may find out lots of bits and pieces of information you never knew. Try not to become too cynical by unsolicited information. People feel the need to unburden themselves of the slightest tidbits of information in an effort to feel vindicated when they choose sides during a divorce and, trust me, they will. This might call into play someone's ability to take certain information with perhaps a pound rather than a grain of salt.

It has taken some time to come to a place in my own life that is tranquil and pleasurable. I am married for a second time to a great man who was never married before. He likes to tease me and say that he was waiting for the right one to come along. I think it was me who was waiting for the right one to come along. Trust me, the right one will come along. Just don't kiss every frog that comes your way. They don't all turn into princes or princesses.

With any luck, my ramblings will give you some insight and allow you to take away something useful from this book. Granted, life is rarely what we expect or planned. Like it or not, we all have to play the ball from where it lies. I don't have your problems and you don't have mine.

I have always had a great deal of difficulty with people who use a bad childhood or the like as an excuse for poor judgment and bad decisions. While these things certainly can play a part in someone's life decisions, we must be responsible for our own actions. So think about your actions and their bearing on an already-complicated situation.

While divorce doesn't make us consciously decide that we'll set out to hurt anyone, let alone our children, it still can happen. I'd like to hope that a smattering of some of the preposterous events in my own life shared here will give some insight into the frightening behavior of which we all are capable—yes, even you.

Never lose sight of the fact that your decisions can and will play a part in your children's choices. Of course, this is true whether you and your spouse divorce or not. A child is not a renewable resource; once ruined, you don't get another chance. There is one chance and one chance only. No Mulligan here.

While the pen may be thought to be mightier than the sword, the spoken word can stab the heart, allowing it to bleed ever so slowly and going unnoticed until it ruins a life. Think of a time in your life that was kinder and gentler and have that be what you bring forth as a parent.

Even as adults, we need validation from our parents. If we have done our job, our children should feel that we support them and find significance in all they endeavor to do. Occasionally, we lose sight of the importance of family, though it's never too late to try to repair any rifts. Time can soothe some wounds, even if they cannot be totally healed. Why not, at the very least, try?

I know that believing people can behave sensibly during a divorce may be a bit of a tall order because, realistically, that is infrequently the case. I dare say we can hope. It is difficult when people seem to come out of the woodwork to tell you things about a spouse—the person you thought you knew everything there was to know about. Understandably, we react, often badly. And while it hurts your heart more than you thought anything could, at the end of the day, they are things you cannot change. Hopefully, those things that don't destroy us make us stronger, and we can move on and make better choices.

You both can agree to disagree about so many things, but agree to give your children the best of each of you that you can. It is your responsibility as a parent to help your children deal with divorce so they know love can be a beautiful emotion. They, too, will make mistakes because we all do. If we learn to own them, learn something from them, and persevere in spite of them, life isn't so bad.

Our home should be the place where we seek solace. Make home, with or without your children's other parent, a respite from life. They, as well as you, need to have a safe haven where you are unburdened from the tempests of life. Divorce can overwhelm us for a time and, for some people, for the rest of their lives. Have respect for yourself and the gift of a child. As we age, it's difficult not to reflect on our contributions to life. There is a realization that we may not have done all we could have. May your legacy be that you've left behind loving, happy memories to be cherished and shared for lifetimes to come.

Oscar Wilde once said, "Children grow to love their parents. Later they judge them, and sometimes they forgive them."

LIFE IS

Life is a precious commodity; minutes tick away into hours, days, months, and years and before we know it, with the grace of God, we are old. For some of us, this is a time to enjoy the remainder of life with our spouse, children, and grandchildren. Sadly, neither of my parents got to do this. I've heard it said that we make plans and God laughs. I believe there is a plan for when we are called to meet our maker, so we must make the best of the time we are allotted.

When we make choices, ones for which we can never reconcile the consequences, we often leave behind people who must deal with the aftermath. In my heart, I know it was not the intent of either of my parents to hurt me, but, in reality, they did. I think they each got so caught up in their own needs that they lost sight of mine. At the same time, it doesn't make it any easier. Nonetheless, it is what it is.

Living is a series of actions and reactions. I'm not sure the next sentence can be said often enough: We need to know for ourselves and in teaching our children that all our actions have consequences. Hopefully, those consequences don't come at too high a cost. We are taught lessons every day;

whether we choose to heed them is another thing. It's important to note that even good people can do stupid things. Most of us are good people. We don't set out to hurt each other or our children, but we still do thoughtless things. Divorces will continue to happen, and we will continue to act foolishly when it comes to their resolutions, though not without consequence.

So at the first sign of problems, put on your best idiot suit, step back, and take a long, long look in the mirror. Do you like what you see? Only you can be a power to change the out come.

So in the end, you are obligated as a parent to make your children into people who can love and respect themselves so they can love and respect others. Obviously, this is an important aspect of parenting, with or without a divorce.

As much as I make an effort to overcome various things my parents may have passed on to me throughout their battles, I recognize I have no control over yesterday. You, as well as I, can make a difference only in tomorrow. Keep this in mind when one or both of you may be winding up for some stunt and the effect it may have on the kids. To quote a scene from the movie *Gandhi*, "Be the change you want to see in the world."

The life each of us has is the legacy we leave. Perhaps we believe most of us have no legacy to bequeath. It is not always about possessions to be dispersed after our death. As a parent, the most important things we leave with our children are our love and concern for their well-being in any circumstance.

When it comes to affairs of the heart, our mind and our spirit do not always act in concert. Love can be an elusive companion. For some of us, relationships seem to never work out quite right and for others, they find that one unwavering soul mate. Society often defines us by our relationship with another person and often judges us when we have failed at one. Perhaps this is why we act out and, for a number of us, act out so unpleasantly at the prospect of our relationship's end.

It seems that during a divorce, there is a no-holds-barred mentality. Family secrets and skeletons are revealed, and provocative information may be shared in inappropriate venues. Ego seems to be the driving force for most of us in this battle of wills. Our sense of self can provoke us to take action with despicable conduct and little regard for the end result.

So much of what you have strived for and worked long and hard to attain may be on the line. Ultimately, it comes down to the two of you vying for money and possessions. Unconsciously, children, more often than not, fit in the lineup somewhere near the bottom. As a result of this mentality, so much unnecessary distress is heaped on everyone affected by a divorce.

Love is an emotion that has everyone in its grasp. The loss of it can cause us to grapple with our inner self and come up with seething thoughts of retribution. In the hurt that can cause us to lose our sense of right and wrong, we first need to understand there is no love that should make us feel like this. It seems obvious that we should understand everyone's life is falling apart for a time—yours, your spouse's, and your children's.

When we have given ourselves the chance to recover and permission to go on, life will move forward. The quality of that life hinges on how the adults involved manage some of the ups and downs. We are each obliged to impart valuable life lessons to our children. Show them life is not about possessions but for the love and concern we have for their well-being.

We must never lose sight of the prize that is our children. May you each achieve love and understanding for yourself and all the things for which you endeavor to accomplish. This is the one reality that will allow each of us to flourish.

In Reality

When divorce becomes an element of your life, there needs to be a strategy. There are those of us who are blindsided when our spouse announces that he or she wants a divorce. Only when we are honest with ourselves, most of us have, at the very least, an inkling that things aren't going well in our relationship. Attorneys, mediators, clergy, whomever we choose to seek advice from, are only liaisons on behalf of our emotions. While consulting one or all of these professionals may be necessary, no one can manage and be in control of the outcome of your life except for you. Use your children as what they are, a catalyst in your journey to a new beginning.

While we may not think of a divorce as a beginning, hanging on to that prospect may help us rally around the whirlpool of swirling emotions. Divorce may possibly be one of, if not the most difficult, the most physically and emotionally exhausting experiences in the lives of all involved. While nothing anyone says makes it easier, trying to keep your wits about you may help in making the conclusion of a divorce as amicable as it can be.

Children, even young children, understand conflict. It is important for them to have meaningful relationships with both of their parents. We cannot allow ourselves to be so out of control that our children no longer feel safe or loved. We need to grow past this, allowing everyone time to take in all the things that are happening.

You may move on easily and never date or marry again. Your spouse, or you for that matter, may already have someone in the wings or may find a new someone quickly, remarry, and possibly have more children. There will be many adjustments for everyone. Whatever each of you chooses to do is not an affront to the other spouse but an endeavor to make a new life. Chess is a game to be mastered, won, or lost. Life is not a game; it cannot be mastered—just lived.

We must learn to embrace life, as it will go on with or without your consent.

EPILOGUE

You know how every snowflake is different? Well, we're all like snowflakes. We think we are the same, but each and every one of us has something that makes us unique.

Just as a snowflake, life seems to disappear in a flash. Our lives are like a layer of the Earth or a ring of a tree. Our responsibility as a parent is to build something of substance day after day. When we as parents have been entrusted with the life of a child, we become the gatekeeper of that life. Individually, we are but a small piece of life, but together we make a family, a generation, and, hopefully, many generations to come. So, yet again, what we do really matters. Divorce only exacerbates the ways in which it matters.

Perhaps we can think of life as an early computer analogy: garbage in, garbage out. The complexities of life can encumber our path. It is our sometimes total disregard and lack of empathy for even our own children that will cause incalculable harm. We each need to step aside for a moment to ensure we will lead a child to become a whole person, a person who can and will make decisions that he or she is content with for a lifetime. In the end, we can only hope that we have helped our children in whatever journey they choose.

As you contemplate or embark on a divorce, remember that forever is a long time. Make the memories you leave behind the ones recalled as fondly as possible.

We can be capable of egregious behavior. Be mindful that there are few times in life when we are able to atone for this sort of behavior. Saying "I'm sorry" doesn't always suffice, even if you are foolish enough to assume so. We may choose to forgive, though forgetting may be another matter all together.

Although I make an effort to keep unpleasant memories at bay, it's not always possible. Sometimes a TV show or something I read can set some childhood memory in motion and even a million years later, I'm in tears. Those instances dredge up an emptiness that makes the distance between age nine and the rest of my life seem very short. When I look back on some of those times when I was growing, it is apparent, though I may try to ignore them, they define who I am. Like it or not, we are a product of those who raised us. The deeds of others and the impact they can and most likely will have on each of us during our lifetimes are infinite

I understand you may be trying to begin a new life that includes a new spouse, new homes, and possibly additional children. None of those things are your kids' problem. You must work out the details before you run headlong into that new life.

While alimony may be an issue between the two of you, child support is not an option but your moral obligation. Perhaps first come, first serve should be the divorce mantra. Keep in mind support is not only about money. You need to be there for your children emotionally as well. That means both of you. Make no mistake, though, providing monetarily for your offspring is your first responsibility.

Remember my father's games with the weekly child support checks? This is yet another example of how adolescent we can behave in divorce situations. Men are not the only ones guilty of these obtuse games, so man up even if you are not the man. Cut the crap and stand up for what we all know in our hearts are the right things to do.

Contentious situations aside, we know what are the right things to do. Some decisions will be made that are not in your favor, but suck it up because that's life. Remember you played a part in you're domestic scenario whether you want to admit it or not. Nothing that happens in a marriage, good or bad, is because of just one of you. Children emulate the adults to whom they are exposed. During the ravaging blows of divorce, we understandably are not always thinking or acting with a clear head. Bad things in life are going to happen. In theory, I guess it's easy to expect that we should be able to sit down and discuss how and what to do regarding what may be best for our lives and our kids. In reality, not so much.

That "honey attracts more bees than vinegar" thing comes to mind and makes sense. Try it out. What's the worst that can happen? Do you really want to stand idly by watching your child's life circle the drain because you and your spouse were too selfish to set aside your own pettiness? Let's face it, if divorce were easy, there wouldn't be so many attorneys, counselors, etc. Most of us with an ounce of sense get it, though it's not always as easy as it sounds. Repeat after me: Actions speak louder than words. A few years down the road, will you be able to look yourself in the mirror and see someone you still like, never mind someone your kids can respect?

Despite the fact that it is so cliché to say, experience is the best teacher. And better days will find their way into your life. Don't let the past dictate who and what you are or deter you from the happiness of moving onward. You know when kids get into petty fights and adults intervene? Fifteen minutes later, the kids are off playing and the adults go on fighting, maybe even for years. I think kids understand life so much more than adults. We might want to stand back and take a lesson.

For myself, it sometimes seems life has been a bit rocky. I long ago came to terms with the times that have scarred my heart, along with the imperfections for which I must take responsibility. I have learned to embrace some of those events I longed to erase as a child and use them to an advantage rather than as a detriment. Life isn't always pretty. Anyone who contradicts this is a liar or thinks you're a fool. Give yourself time to heal. The rest really does fall into place, if you let it.

While not perfect, my life is a compilation of the good and less-than-great times that have brought me both pleasure and discontent. But when looking back on them, it makes me realize how fortunate I am to have had that ride. We all struggle until we appreciate those events for what they really are. They are the means for us to find the person who helps make all those wrongs right.

And finally, I have.

A Few Personal Notes

To my mother and father: I hope each of you has found peace. Daddy, I'm sure when you met up with Mom, she kicked your ass. I guess you both did the best you could under the circumstances; the rest was up to me.

Thank you to my ex-husband: While our marriage did not end up as either of us planned, it allowed me to have a child not by biology but through the bond of love.

My deepest love to you, the child of my heart: Thank you for allowing me to continue to have a place in your life and now that of your children. We have been a learning experience for each other, and my life is richer for your part in it.

And finally to my husband: Yes, the second time is lovelier. If I had been able to put my order in with God, I could not have been sent a better person to teach me what love really is about.

I hope each of you finds the same.

About the Author

Ellen Shaker has long been concerned about the effect divorce has on children. Her perspective as a child of divorce, a stepchild, and a stepparent and having been divorced sheds light on the issues created by divorce. These pages attempt to point out the things that, while apparent to us all, we still ignore when it comes to the game of divorce. In sharing personal experiences, she hopes to convey the importance of how adults can better prepare both themselves and their children for a divorce. How we play our own game of divorce is as important as how we finish that game.

Ellen grew up and was educated in Cheshire, Connecticut. She and her husband live in New Milford, Connecticut. They have two grandchildren, who are the children of Ellen's stepson.

She is embarking on a new career in speaking engagements and collaboration with local mediators on the subject of divorce. Please direct inquiries to 203-470-9238.